The Real Moon of Poetry
and Other Poems

tina brown celona

Cover painting by   Renee van der Stelt

Author Photo by   Matt Celona

Published in the United States by   Fence Books
                                     14 Fifth Avenue, #1A
                                     New York, NY 10011
                                     www.fencebooks.com

Book design by   Fence Books

Fence Books are distributed by   University Press of New England
                                     www.upne.com

Printed in Canada by   Westcan Printing Group
                                     www.westcanpg.com

Library of Congress Cataloguing in Publication Data
Tina Brown Celona [1974–]
The Real Moon of Poetry and Other Poems / Tina Brown Celona

Library of Congress Control Number: 2002111805

ISBN 0-9713189-3-X

First Edition

Grateful acknowledgment to *Epoch, Explosive!*, Katy Lederer and
Spectacular Books, Rebecca Wolff and *Fence*, to all my teachers, to my
parents, and to Matt, Katherine, David, Justine, Mike and Josh.

for matt

table of contents

Pastorale 1

Dream 2

Hiroshima 3

The Big Day 5

The Office in Wartime 6

Discovery 7

To Say a Man 8

Emotion 9

Spectacular Emotion 10

The Medium 13

Days 14

Malaise 15

A Poem Without a Camel 16

Angry? No 19

Camera 20

Our Youth 21

Sincerity 22

"If It All Went Up in Smoke" 24

Kosovo 25

Fin de Siecle 26

The Harvesters 27

The Sky 28

Five Difficulties 29

Love 32

Jade Rabbit 33

A Song for the Moon 34

Poem 35

Narrative 36

Dakota 37

The Adolescent 38

In My Beginning 39

On Saturday 40

Notes 41

Event 43

The Waitress Diaries 44

Farm 46

It's Good to Get Away Now & Then 49

Fantastic Heart 52

Poet Sex 54

Sentences 57

Pastorale

Let us look at it another way. The scream seemed to come from across the meadow. Taking our notebooks, we set out across the field, turning over stones, looking for the source of the scream. We wrote, a thing has screamed. The screaming continued. We wrote, the screaming continues. Under our feet the grass, the grass of the horse field, caused us to stumble. We stumble, we wrote, walking across the field. The horses, in the woods by the water, moved uneasily towards the road. A car went by, then another. Another goes by in the poem. A car goes by. The river is still, a light wind touches it, a few leaves float down from the trees.

Dream

My dream scuttles up the trunk of an areca palm.
It has six feet like the mice of my childhood.
I am ashamed to acknowledge it.
It cries out to the world for attention.
My body, at the foot of the palm, is blue.
The soles of its feet weep. These two, my dream and my body,
exist to plague one another. The shriveled organ of my
       imagination
hangs from a frond, tosses with the breeze.
I curl and uncurl my long arm.
I am an octopus
squeezed between two flowerpots.

Hiroshima

1.

After the smoke had cleared
After the dust had settled, the ash
Drifting slowly across the roofs,
A little tinsel, some coins, artillery shells
Glittered in the rubble.
The student, gazing in disbelief
At the eye in his hand
Could not have been prepared
Though he had copied the books
Page by page into his journals. These
He searched for now
Under the stones of the house
Where minutes before
Even shadows had halted
Forever embroidered
By the Singer sewing machine
Dropped from the sky.

2.

That day the owls hooted derisively
Their beaks perforated with seed-sized holes.
At the ruined museum
Icarus tumbled like a mouse into the waves.
At last the cartoons of the subconscious

Rose into the sky,
Inflating the teeth of the collapsed vinyl
God, fur-lined teacup
Held to its lips. A flock of buzzsaws
Bear down on a painting
Fragments of plaster gliding inertly
Into the skull of the Jew
Pinned to the door of the church, an orange
Clutched between his jaws, one shoe
Dropping into the street
Where weeds exchange genes
Like a movie run backwards. We have remembered
To wear our old clothes, but the rain
Falls through them too. Put the world back
Where it was, Commissioner. The shrimp
Cry out for justice
From the seafloor, leaving tiny trails,
Traces of poetry.

The Big Day

Helplessly   in the bright air
Dreaming of war
The President wakes. The cameras are ready
And waiting. The President climbs into the cab
Of a big green tractor and
Waves to the angry populace.
He honks the horn and flashes the lights
To applause. "New-cular," he whispers
Happily. America is a great country.
Everyone else had better
Watch out!

The Office in Wartime

1.

When the war started the words started.
They melted like snow
On the cloth of war.
In the midst of the avalanche
The fax machine printed a menu
And one of the potted palms
Turned brown and died.
Someone wrote a poem.
Someone else tried to hit a fly
With a rolled-up magazine and missed
And was relieved.

2.

She is the personal trainer.
By the pool they hit each other.
Everyone wonders if
There will be a war. If God will
Help us. The pool sparkles
Like freedom.

Discovery

He is writing a magnificent poem about the world. It began
being about the world but gradually now it turns into the
world. Bees and slugs crawl about in the letters. The letters
become ants, then flies which are eaten by birds. The birds
are in turn eaten by larger birds, who take them out of the air,
or by snakes, who slither up to their nests. It is nesting time
for the birds, the air is pink and green, then blue and orange,
now suddenly the leaves shrivel and fly, it is once again win-
ter. The letters are invisible, sinking into the layer of leaves
and wet earth. The ground freezes, the river is visible from
the house. Things in their possibility appear, reappear, are
still, disappear. The snow falls. Birds fight over seeds, which
are once again letters. A barred owl drops after a mouse,
which that moment turns into a letter. The snow, gently
falling, covers the ground, the seed-table, with letters. In the
distance, across the river, deer stumble along a path, searching
for straw, bits of dry grass. They find only letters. Fish at the
bottom of the river swim up through the letters. The letters of
the river spell "water" and "wet" and "river." On the surface,
"ice." Trees are legible in the distance. The eye lingers on the
page. The page lingers in the eye.

To Say a Man

To say a man walks down a road
is not false
somewhere   a man walks down a road
up a driveway into a house
in autumn
if there are leaves on the ground
summer if on the trees
a man walks under

Emotion

My emotion was very small. It was the emotion of a poem. It was made of words, it could be taken apart as words could be taken apart into letters. The letters of my emotion spoke for me. You are sad, they said, you are crying, they said, you do not want to look at the trees, you are tired of your beautiful books. Surely my tears were real? They are real, said the words, as real as the words. I am tired of words, I said. Take out your tongue, they replied. I took out my tongue but the words spoke for me as before. Take out your eyes, they suggested. I took out my eyes but the words spoke in my ear. Cut off your ears, the words whispered. When I had cut off my ears, the words moved in my head like a worm. Describe us, they said.

Spectacular Emotion

for Josh

all the emotion is spectacular
all the—emotion
is a firework going off   just for you

today i found a postcard it said i love you
if even postcards love me i guess
i can do anything
our poems are almost over
real life is coming on
like it was never here
your new voice
just words falling
out

xxxxxxkkKXXXXxxxx is what
i would like to do to you and the
world

let us become our pauses
let us become our parents
let us write new poems for the new poem industry
the sun like god
smug and stupid   the rules like god
the snake in our muscle
have a cookie or a cookie cutter
they were on the bench
the river of sun down the street
pulling my eyes out of line

you were in the window like
max jacob yelling to picasso
come back or go home
i will destroy all your paintings

everyone is dead there is no looking for
them in the stream the giant vulva
breaking off in the current   dearest and
darling with tears in her eyes—pleading

out of the garden

i remember nothing. it is an expense
he is a big yell. where were we going to go
how could we go without
before this fight
changing everything. as you say it is
possibly hypothetical
but then we are also not there
some more words like sprinkles

the world is stupid! i   hate   it
and myself in it   poem after poem
i have no existence apart from. if
we could make our poems true
we could go back
to them. bringing them
across time is no answer.

you will never get away from me unless
i let you. juliana spahr or not

"sometimes you make me so mad"
pronouncing anyone
a theoretical question
of course you are only in my heart
my only heart to be in

which i wrote to prove
anything could go
my name in code on the cover of this
anthology of very modern poetry
your voice going out
like a sentimental light
my emotion is also spectacular
my tears have tears
and i wipe them off with poems.
no one is going to teach you patience
sex is an impostor

like these photos of frank stanford
we can't send back
                    —the guilt, the guilt
my sanity is charming

The Medium

Nature had disappeared in a laugh. It could still be found, at the edges of cities, clinging to images. Further away it became "landscape." Gradually the images became real, as real as nature had been. We saw ourselves in the images. We stepped into the mirror. On the other side of the mirror was death. Death moved backwards; a wind blew, moving us. We wept; we stretched our arms toward the mirror. In the mirror we saw ourselves moving away. We painted the mirror; we painted ourselves in the mirror. The poem became an eye. Weeping, it gazed into the mirror. The mirror was there, there in the eye. What the eye saw came toward the mirror. Behind us were trees. The trees in the mirror grew leaves. We saw ourselves walking under the trees. We saw ourselves painting the leaves.

Days

The days are like a row of corpses
Face down at the edge of a pit.
One by one I turn them over
And kick them in.
I do not bother to remove
Their wedding rings.
I do not count their teeth. I stare
Them straight in the eye,
Like a crow.

Malaise

Suddenly what is required is genius, not
talking about it. "We"
re-existed. A rash — hives, or a cluster of spider bites — spread
from my jaw, under my ear, to just
where my lip
was disappearing in a cosmic
attempt to be, or an attempt to be cosmic. Without
memory, we are left with the moment. After the moment
has passed, only pleasure — a globe of flowers
half-chewed, naturally wilted, on the card table.

A Poem Without a Camel

I thought I could write a poem without a camel so I left mine at home. As I was writing my poem my camel appeared at the window. I took it home and tied it to the fence. As I returned to my poem I felt free of the camel. But the camel was there, looking in at the window. I took the camel to the zoo and left it with the other camels. When I returned to my poem I detected a whiff of camel in the air. I scrubbed my poem with vinegar but the camel was hard to get off. Fearing that the camel would escape from the zoo, I closed the window and sealed it with tape. I turned back to my poem. The room was hot and airless, but at least it was free of the camel. I continued writing my poem, looking around now and then to see if the camel had returned. A camel appeared at the window but it was not my camel. Nevertheless I covered the window with newspaper. It was hot and dark and I could hardly breathe but I continued writing my poem. Finally I finished. My hands were shaking and I was short of breath but I was satisfied that I had managed to keep the camel out of my poem. I reread the poem. No camel. I turned it over to make sure that the camel wasn't hiding behind it. I scrutinized what I thought might be a camel footprint but it was only a little dirt. Dripping with sweat I uncovered the window and opened it. Sunlight and air flooded the room. From across the city I thought I heard my camel sneezing forlornly after me. We had never been apart, my camel and I. Just to be sure I took my poem to a specialist. Shaking his head, he confirmed that the poem was indeed camel-free. Certificate in hand, I went back to the zoo to pick up my camel. I was very tired and happy. I stood at the gate and whistled for my camel. Several other camels ran over but my camel was nowhere to be seen. Could it have escaped, I wondered. I went home, expecting to see my camel waiting for me by the fence. I went back to my office but it was dark and empty and smelled of vinegar. I returned to the zoo which was about to close for the night. Sadly I whistled again for my camel. Several camels came over but my camel was not among them. Where is my camel? I asked the zookeeper, who was sweeping up camel droppings. Which one was yours? answered the zookeeper. It occurred to me that I might not have recognized my camel among so many. I whistled again and the camels came over. I made the special sound I make to my camel. Several of the camels sneezed, but the sneezes all sounded alike. It was getting late and the zookeeper wanted to close. You can come back tomorrow, he suggested. On the way home I thought wistfully of the happy times my camel and I had shared. A tear trickled down my cheek as I remembered the day I had brought him home from the camel dealer. I looked unhappily at my poem and at my certificate of authenticity. That night I slept very little. In the morning I headed back to the zoo. Have you seen my camel? I asked the zookeeper. It wasn't at home? he replied. No, I said sadly. How about another camel, the zookeeper suggested. It wouldn't be the same, I replied. Sadly I returned to my office. I wrote a poem and then another poem about my camel, but without my camel the poems seemed empty. Something was missing and I suspected it was the camel. I took out my poem from the day before and compared it to the new poems I had written. The camel was missing from all of them. I turned back to my poems but my heart wasn't in it. I thought, it was foolish to have wanted to write a poem without a camel. As the weeks wore on I wrote an entire book of poems without a camel, and then another. Then I stopped writing entirely.

Angry? No

Just hungry

Just lonely
Your ocean of skin includes me
Bashing on the rocks of the bed
The cliffs of the
Seabed the
Poem twisting like a
Tornado over the
Plains of the interior
Decoration

Camera

The warmth of your lap
Is close enough to love
So I climb in. Steadily
you look at me.
Like an endless
Camera.

Our Youth

It is said the simple cannot deceive But
that is philosophy
Loose ends of a painting
causing the faculties to idle.
Where there was no you
a whole temperament
provided the representation
of an animal gazing
at a copy of sky. Dark water
appeared, red-veiled insects
A drowned mouse. Where with one
motion the object of
countless syntheses was revealed.
You and I, two innumerables
among the wastes of Poland, fields
of burnt cornstalks
The yellow surface of the mind.

Sincerity

We follow the boy across a field where cows are grazing.
We cross a road and then another.
The fields stretch out in every direction.
A heavy cloud moves westward across the sky, towards the
    town in the distance.
The town lies at a crossroads.
The corn in the fields is knee-high.
A truck moves along the road to the north of the town.
The sky is blue, high, and perfectly clear.
As the boy approaches the house, two cats sitting by the door
    run under the hedge.
The contrails of a plane are barely visible to the southeast.
Behind the house, the river passes between a field and a wood.
The sun is warm and the grass especially green.
The truck has reached the town and has stopped there.
A chicken detaches itself from the truck and runs clucking into
    the street.
Within seconds it is hit by a Volvo.
The Volvo continues toward the east, eventually leaving
    the town.
The boy disappears into the house.
The truck moves along the road to the south of the town.
It is passed by a car going in the opposite direction.
The car continues towards the town.
The truck moves along the road to the north of the town.
The sky is high, blue, and perfectly clear.
Within seconds it is hit by a Volvo.
The Volvo continues along the road to the east of town.

The fields stretch out in all directions.
The sun is warm and the grass especially green.
The corn in the fields is knee-high.
A chicken detaches itself from the truck and runs clucking into
       the cornfield.
We continue along the road to the north of the town.
A plane passes over, slightly to the west.
The fields stretch out in every direction.

"If It All Went Up in Smoke"
after Oppen

The field of color—
Walls
white walls, the Satisfaction
Of air
First glassed-in
It had been torn down.

In your hair, mouth
The poem washes its pants.
Pattern
Vertical, silent
Snow on the larch, the window
applied in paint-panes
Opens toward

The unconcerned
Classic light.

Kosovo

The painting, like the sea, reaches outward
Into nature. Not enough is visible
But the edge of the sea
of the painting must edge
What cannot certainly be called art. By her fifth book
She had discovered an objection
To the use of the first person plural
And to adjectives
Furnishing forth
Unsuggestively the equivalent of color
Applied, like hope and sleep,
To compensate us for the miseries of life. But who,
she asked herself, was us? The mind
rose, expanding
Moonlike above the gutters, piloted
as if by the release of an enormous egg
from the immense ovary
of the dispersed nuclear cloud. If the two chairs
on the painted stairs were
Out of all scale, the frame, four-fifths "sky,"
Was at least more reasonable, more
conceivable, than the air we "breathed,"
it was our right to breathe. To think, being pulled under
and returned again to the surface, of
the eyes of the villagers, of their eyeless sons.
Away from the field, checking his watch
The color of flowers
Mechanically
Enters the view.

Fin de Siecle

It is not really a matter of good or bad
The two chairs mounted
on the bleached and painted canvas. The artist
is gone, was here, is gone. In any
of the many conceivable emptinesses something
has been painted over. Behind the paint, one can assume
something is hidden —
one cannot assume nothing is hidden. A bit of blue
stuck in among the meticulously
abbreviated hair. "It is a painting
of a closet
invaded by mice. The little brown spots
you see to the bottom right of the canvas
are not — as expected — mouse turds, but
painted grains of rice."

The Harvesters

The moon of the lamp
A small mirror flashing
Again off blue snow.

In the field of harvesters, who are the lovers?
The blue church
Is given the magnificent sky
The blue concrete, the melting snow.

The mirror shrinks
Into the wheat field
Is ground to
Silver flour.

There, a symbol. Mouth and tongue
Of an animal
Obscured by darkness. A hundred letters
Dissolve like pigeon wings
Bursting from their crib
Into a familiar sky.

My second wife
Carries our clothes to the river,
Returns smiling.

The Sky

An opportunistic sincerity
Deprived of
Its scenery
Tended to discourage those
Who saw it
Was "not-seeable"
Under the Birthday cake
And yet the figure
Half-turned toward
The ruins—waving her hand
Confirmed in distance
Said nothing—could not say
"I am the accident"

Five Difficulties

1.

That day I did not write
The poem came closer
I asked him, I said to the poet
—or I wanted to ask
I wanted to get over
my fear. And then from
behind us the rattle
of a bird in *Some Trees*.

2.

Letters come from the sea
where it is quiet
but for the noise
You cannot hear here.
A tropical storm, moving
north, left traces of salt
from the Gulf. Like the poet's
mother I believe I did not
know in my bones
what to do.

3.

The poet has no mother
And the sea is not particular
It washes up
Goes out
From the continent, from Alaska.
When the visiting
poet was helping me
I was helping myself. How painfully
I think of myself.

4.

I could not sleep.
I was afraid I would kill myself if I were alone.
The moon was blurred.
The wooden cat was spotted and painted with flowers.
I thought of the graveyard, then thought
Might I not have thought of another. In the gloom I thought
I could make out my life. You were
At the beach, you said, you went there often.

5.

But our love, you said.
It is only a tin can, I replied.
But our vows, you said.
They are only paper.
I am off to California.
There I will buy a car.
I will live alone in a house
until the money runs out.
I will write poems
until I die. I will die,
I will die, I will die.

Love

1.

If you are near, there you are,
I want to touch you.
And bite your face.
When I sleep, when I wake up
You are there.
Our toothbrush is pink
In the morning we go to the store
And look at the terns.

2.

You can take away
This house, you can quietly
Work on poems
The beach is there, the sea birds
Tumble through the air
Glide along
Beaks underwater. You can take away
The bed, the breeze
Drifting. A man sleeping
Like the number four.
Summer full of hope
Like a boat with a sail.

Jade Rabbit

i consider writing about something
i have written about before
but am interrupted by something outside
very wet because of the rain
and it occurs to me i will never
say convincingly, "let's go swimming"
because you know i don't like swimming
though we go often but because
i always say "so should we go
swimming" doubtfully
looking at my jade rabbit
his humid color and placid posture
as he nibbles the orange ground
of a book by john ashbery,
rivers and mountains

A Song for the Moon

the moon is more beautiful
later
when i have gone to bed
with my poem
about the moon

with my beautiful poem
about the beautiful moon
in my poem

the real moon looks real
too real for my poem

the moon in my poem
is better
for poetry

the real moon of poetry
is better for me

Poem

A man heard his wife yelling in another room.
Let me out! Let me out! yelled the wife.
The curtains at the windows of the room were yellow
But the rug and the walls were no color
Just as the air was no color.
Let us continue this a little while longer,
Said the husband. He is looking for
A poem in the *New York Times*.
"Help, help," screams his wife.
Unfortunately a prophet is screaming at the same time
Both victims are in flames,
The man is sitting calmly on his sofa reading.
In his loneliness he swims farther into the dark lake
And his head is a hive of feeling.
"You, there, why don't you take off your underpants?"
He calls to a young woman sunning herself on the bank.
She leaps up indignantly
Why can't today be like yesterday, he mutters bitterly
Thinking of his incinerated wife.

Narrative

Snow fell, attaching to and wetting the plate glass window, beyond which the white masts of watercraft were visible. The fireplace was like a mouth in the wall, and he filled it with wood and a little paper. He thought, it is not a dream, but a book of dreams. He corrected himself:

She looked at the people on the train. The windows flashed, now black, now charcoal, now a white cross-hatching, now sky above a river. She thought, if I refer to myself as "He," it will seem less personal.

My mouth was full of stones. A garden grew from the stones, and a green tongue flapped soundlessly within.

There is a mother, and a father, and a sister. They are fires in a snowfield. Snow falls into them, and before the tiny leaves appear on the black shrubs, one of the fires will collapse, sink, and disappear under the falling snow.

Dakota

The little leaves on the trees sparkle.
I move the plant
To the bedroom window
As I would move you
To a bedroom window of poetry.

What are we waiting for?
We are waiting for approbation.
I saw the swans by the pond
Dipping their gorgeous necks
In silence. The cardinal
Like a red sock
In the juniper bush

Articulates the secret:
The difficulty, that is:
Looking good naked.

The Adolescent

When I heard that my poem
had been showing off
I took out all its words.

When I heard that my poem
had been making a scene
I took out all its emotion.

When my poem was nothing
I heard nothing about it
So I went on vacation.

When I came back from vacation I
heard that my poem
was packing to leave

So I cancelled its tickets.
You are no fun, said my poem
and you are making me miserable.

You are nothing but trouble, I said
See if anyone else
will put up with you.

In the morning my poem
was gone. When I heard
of my poem again

it was dead. I was angry, I said.

In My Beginning

I am ready to write the poem
Now that I am wearing your sweater
Your letter sweater
The poem that renounces poetry:

I believe she is in Kyoto
Where the dead poodles lie.

Shall we
Sprinkle our poems with nouns
That remind us of Nature?
Shall we lie down in our yards
And cover ourselves with dirt?

Hear the tango in the hall.
It is the easiest thing of all
To sing tippling-songs at dawn, to say
"Your poem does not amuse us,
Let us throw it away."

On Saturday

You try to convince me
Our tree is telling us
It doesn't want to wear Christmas lights.

I remind God that all I want
Is to write poems.
God tells me I don't know
What's good for me,
Sits on my chest
Poking his penis in my face.

Notes

❄

Sleeping inside
We rarely see the moon
Unless we live in a skyscraper
And it is at eye level.

❄

Hurrying   to get the poem.
And another one, falling
To the ground like parachutes
In a video game.

❄

The cat   nervously sleeping.
I smell her ear;
It smells all right. The spider
in the window is frozen.
So are the bugs.

❄

From where I sit at my desk I look for
Your orange helmet
But it is only the hood of a red car.
My heart beats
Like its blinker.

❋

Every weekend it is he
Who stages the fight
Does he want me
to leave him? And not know how
to Prosecute it?
Leave my garden? And this miraculous
Poem-recognizer?

❋

The poem there   was a record of movement
From me to you
Cat, and the birds

❋

Lazily I put my banana peel   on the phone

Event

My hands at the ends of my arms
Come closer
They are brown
And heavily veined. My fingers
Tremble a little, waiting
For me to put them away.
Like an insect my cat
Flies up to my lap.
My cat does not know
I have not yet written a poem.
The birds concern her.
She watches them from the window
Only her tail moving.

The Waitress Diaries

"That terrible day my heart took a blow that nearly killed it."
I give myself until eleven. I don't feel like going to work. I
don't want to leave until the last possible second. How long
will it take me to buy a blow dryer? I don't know. I decide to
get the cat food on my way home. The garage door opens.
There is someone inside after all. I will have to hurry.

These are my thoughts. Great,
No one can understand.
I am going to the park.
Soon I will forget all about it.

Can I have my job back?

The waitress jiggles the baby on her hip. The baby is sucking a
pacifier. It looks at me and its head wobbles.

Where are you? You are at the paint store. I will not bother
you with my emotions.
Where are you? You are planting potatoes. The paint is yellow
and you apply it like a technician. You apply it with precision.

One thing is certain: I would make a terrible waitress.

We talk about school. I do not say anything about my problem. I have nothing more important to do than talk to you, I say sincerely. I'm looking forward to summer. If I did nothing else I would love you. We fight to see who is a better person. Sometimes you let me win. I play the best words but I do not get the most points.

They called it that because they wanted to imply that women's poetry is like an extraordinary tide. It cannot be stopped. It is female like the ocean.

I go to bed at noon. When I crawl out of bed I see you standing in the doorway with your hat in your hand. Hello, cowboy, I say. I am just kidding. I will never know which people ordered which entree. Waitressing seems easier when it is not your job.

The pink bottle is on my lap. It is blue with pink fur. We do not walk around in the evening. You are not painting it yellow. Are you spraying the aphids? R U spraying near the aphids?

Farm

It is not that kind of farm — Old MacDonald–style — for one thing it is organic — everything is organic even the fertilizer — it is entirely run by men — men with beards, men with pencil heads, men in overalls — it is not an abstract farm — it is real — and now the wood thrush is making its watery sound and the rhubarb is raising thick flowers to the sun — and now my organic pear (not from the farm) is making me fart, or maybe it is the chocolate-chip pie — in a few hours you will be home — smelling of fish emulsion perhaps and dirt — the smell of which clings to my hands having seeped permanently into the little crevices next to my nails — for a day of labor — we ought to have more group dinners — not necessarily vegan — I wonder if farting is a sign of gastrointestinal distress — distress over the pie — distress over chocolate — the sun coming over the wall at the same time every morning — regular — so shall we go — away to the (throbbing) city — shall we — take our chances — look for work — like innumerable people before us — I am not pleased with my dress it is not exactly as we had expected — but I do love my lemon colored sweater because it was so expensive — can you guess how expensive — well it was insanely expensive — to begin with but it had been marked down twice — but about the farm — there is absolutely nothing like it — you cannot go to a museum and find it — the mailman cannot deliver it — you can write poems about it but it is better not to — carrots — salad — brassicas — weeding, hoeing, planting — all farm activities — if we go to the city it will be like starting over — we have done it before — but now we are older — does anyone — need an executive secretary — I

am not quite—executive enough—the flowers—at the farm
are plentiful—in August—the bees—pollinate the apple trees
but not the strawberries in our yard—the ospreys are nesting
every kind of bird is nesting, or calling to its mate—the gur-
gling wren—the ha-ha of the jay—and this morning the
woodpecker's surprise appearance at the feeder—oh how my
voice—tires me—the noise of increase—to which we owe—
our very existence the subway—crash of trains the sewers
the streets not roads as we have here in the country—Time is
merciless—my sweater—is actually lemon meringue col-
ored—I was about to say—covered—lightly comic—darkly
lucid—my poems—I think—this dress is totally out of the
question—covering as it barely does my chest—that is my
breasts—unfortunately they have centered the lily on my
poitrine—I do not have a tan—my shoulders are scarred
from pimples—I put it on anyway it will be the first thing you
see when you walk in the door—how it looks like—it is
pulling off my tits—face it, a strapless—is not something
everyone can wear—especially one that is held up by an elas-
tic band that compresses one's tits and pulls them down—I'm
telling you—there's nothing uglier than a girl with ugly tits—
cows have four—cows live on farms—you see where I'm
going with this, back to the farm—wouldn't it be embarrass-
ing if my dress slipped off my tits—at the wedding with
everyone watching—turning away—being revolted—if I
look down—I can see my tummy pooching out—I think—it
is absolutely out of the question—when are you going to
come home—my other dress—shows off my muscles—when

am I going to see you approaching like an orange bug—
and then the yellow of the bike—and then the blue of the
bag—that's how I see you—I'm freezing—in this dress—my
hair is perfect—suddenly everyone is rediscovering their
blow dryer—this dress—barely covers my nipples, though
it's true that my nipples are very big—I remember telling
Mary having you read The Waitress Diaries was like
taking off all my clothes and then you telling me I'm ugly—
by the way—I killed a rice moth today—they must have
gotten into the oats—or woken up after winter—anyway—
We are going to have an infestation, you remind me

It's Good to Get Away Now and Then

1.

This is a great time of year.
Is there a "there" there
In the photograph
Of a meadow
Glistening with dew?
Look closer: You can see a spider
In the grass. You can see its red mandibles
As it gnaws a bug.
The bug has pages.

2.

More slowly now, yet it goes on. We are back in the landscape
of letters. The pages of a book, a book of elegant pictures,
turn in the wind, releasing bits of gold leaf to the wind. It is
winter, judging by the snow. It is too bad, but it can't always
be summer. The corpses of rats lie in the corners where they
crawled after ingesting the Vitamin D. Don't feel bad, it is
only a photograph. It is a photograph of a mirror sucking on
his face. It is like a Gorgon the way it sucks on his face. I
liked her because her legs were powerful.

3.

Let's not use the word "landscape" in a poem.
And especially not the word "poem." Why do we use these
words in a poem?
If I told you I'd have to kill you.

4.

After all they were pale and faded. They smelled like dust. I
did not feel that he owed me anything. I wanted to be up there
with them. It's very early for you, they said. It spread across
the wall of the shed. I spoke frothingly of her cigarette.

5.

It is not the text
He writes in French, English
Photograph, dust, mirrors,
Language, mouth, city, pages,
River of (stone, or perhaps
By *At Passages* he was already
Imitating himself)
Looking into windows the police

Drive slowly by.
The most European of American poets
Serious, diabolical
Mr. Is-Was himself.

Fantastic Heart

1.

My eyes focused more slowly
As if I were swimming.
I am not a horrible girl, I repeated.
No, I am smart and beautiful
And nice and thoughtful
And interesting and special
And noble and delightful.

2.

That little girl
Leaning over the bear is not me.
They are lying on placemats
And are covered with brown
Paper towels. Like most children,
And unlike most insects,
She has almost no torso.

3.

You are just doing it to be outrageous, he says
And I am a little ashamed that this is so.
The pain of stopping is continual though
So I go on telling him I am

In the process of killing myself.
I just want to be a vegetable, I insist,
A humorous, attractive vegetable that goes well
With any meat.

3.

Stay on your side, said the little boy
To the little girl
Riding the orange noodle.
We grieved; the day was terminating;
We had peonies in the seams of our underwear.

4.

I won't feel bad when it's over, I remind myself,
Looking at the picture of the child gazing into
A cake twice the size of her face.

Suddenly I am looking into her horrible,
Immense vagina.
It is just beginning to rain.

Poet Sex

1.

He could see her mouth saying the words. He was observing her carefully and her chin was moving up and down, up and down. She was almost chewing the words, he observed, so he asked her to stop. It was too much, those lips masticating and caressing and devouring the words, letter by letter.

Later he felt like touching her on her vagina. He imagined himself touching her on her vagina which was hairy on top and slippery at the bottom. He could see her masticating the words and hear himself repeating them in his high thin voice, like a speech therapist:

"Goldfish only go
To a certain depth, he said. He said
That if the food fell to the bottom it was too low
And probably wouldn't be eaten," she said.
He told himself it was just a suggestion.

"'I thrust the poem like a gun into my panties,'
He said," she said.
"Nobody laugh," he said, "or I'll blow you to smithereens."

2.

At that moment I felt my head-muscle's
Unearthly strength. I could feel it throbbing
Like a motorcycle motor.
I dare you   to touch me, he said,
Unzipping his pants. I too can be a sex goddess

Without confessing everything. I do not have orgasms,
          she admitted,
During sex. He was secretly appalled,
Though he flexed the muscle of his genius.

3.

He went for a long, satisfying run in the afternoon.
It was happening to her almost against her will.
I can do this as well as anyone, she told herself.

"Everybody happy in there?" she said
Leaning over the fishbowl.

4.

"I would say that, overall, there was not much sexual
        feeling
Between us," she said. No one has ever spoken so frankly
        about sex.

It is almost too much to bear. "I get a thought in my mind,
Her wet nose in my nostril,
The puckering of her anus. I too have a raunchy side,"
She said. He could see her masticating the words.
Hair covered her pimply neck.

5.

They spent the morning together in silence. Afterwards she
could not remember what they had talked about or even
whether they had talked. Had it been a series of cliches? Had
anyone, in fact, said anything? She felt neutral. Are you con-
centrating? he asked her. She was looking out the window.
He could tell she was thinking about the mouth of speech.

Sentences

The worship of the imagination was over.
From the outset I strove above all to be honest, to report
     faithfully the facts
As I had encountered, as I encountered them.
"Rain falls in the poem," I wrote. "It is like looking
     into Nature."
Plowing, horses, all were as words bursting from the dead
     branches of poetry.
On the branch above us a dove hissed. The river flashed
My head was a cloud.
In the meadow of the poem I planted flowers invisible
     to the naked eye.
"Syntax," I explained, "is the breath of poetry."
Belief did not feel like a fact.
I came to believe, after all, in what seemed to be real.
The meadow, I believed, was real.
Through the boards I could see a moon made of paper.
On it I made out words to a song—
Ordinary, contentious words.

FENCEbooks

The Real Moon of Poetry and Other Poems
Tina Brown Celona
2002 ALBERTA PRIZE

The Red Bird
Joyelle McSweeney
2002 FENCE MODERN POETS SERIES

Can You Relax in My House
Michael Earl Craig

Zirconia
Chelsey Minnis
2001 ALBERTA PRIZE

Miss America
Catherine Wagner

About **FENCE**books

FENCE was launched in the spring of 1998. A biannual journal of poetry, fiction, art and criticism, *Fence* has a mission to publish challenging writing distinguished by idiosyncrasy and intelligence rather than by allegiance with camps, schools, or cliques. *Fence* has published works by some of the most esteemed contemporary writers as well as excellent writing by the completely unknown. It is part of our mission to support young writers who might otherwise have difficulty being recognized because their work doesn't answer to either the mainstream or to accepted modes of experimentation.

FENCEbooks is an extension of that mission: With our books we provide expanded exposure to poets and writers whose work is excellent, challenging, and truly original.

The Alberta Prize is an annual series administered by Fence Books in collaboration with the Alberta duPont Bonsal Foundation. The Alberta Prize offers publication of a first or second book of poems by a woman, as well as a five thousand dollar cash prize.

Our second prize series is the **Fence Modern Poets Series**. This contest is open to poets of either gender and at any stage in their career, be it a first book or fifth, and offers a one thousand dollar cash prize in addition to book publication.

For more information about either prize, visit our website at **www.fencebooks.com**, or send an SASE to Fence Books/[Name of Prize], 14 Fifth Avenue, #1A, New York, NY 10011.

For more about *Fence,* visit **www.fencemag.com**.

WITHDRAWN